CEN 5/12

Black

Little Murders Everywhere

REBECCA MORGAN FRANK

salmonpoetry

Published in 2012 by
Salmon Poetry
Cliffs of Moher, County Clare, Ireland
Website: www.salmonpoetry.com
Email: info@salmonpoetry.com

ISBN 978-1-907056-89-5

COVER ARTWORK: *Rosamond Purcell,* Ephemera
COVER DESIGN: *Siobhán Hutson*

For my parents

Acknowledgments

Grateful acknowledgment is made to the editors of the following publications in which these poems, some in slightly different form, first appeared::

Barn Owl Review, "Even the Galaxies"
Birmingham Poetry Review, "Notes to the Scientist"
Calyx, "Song of the Rattling Pipes"
Center, "Railroad Apartment"
The Cincinnati Review, "Cityscape" and "Mire"
Cream City Review, "Gemini"
DQM, "Dialectic"
Eclipse, "An Everyday Disaster"
Eleven Eleven, "Watershed Ghazal"
Fugue, "Celestial Mechanics" and "Infestation"
Grub Street Free Press, "For the Sin of Lying"
The Georgia Review, "For the Sin of Foolishness"
The Guardian Poetry Workshop, "How to Skin a Swan"
Locuspoint, "For the Sin of Two-timing," "After Vietnam," and "Manual Alphabet"
Museum of Fine Arts, Boston 2007 Jewish Film Festival Program: "For the Solitary Diner"
Notre Dame Review, "Rescuer," and "For the Sin of Forgetting"
Passages North, "Residential"
Phoebe, "Aftermath"
Poetry Center of Chicago 15th Juried Reading Chapbook, "Eros is Headed Towards Us"
Post Road, "The Blessing of the Animals," "Wheels," and "Local Carnival"
Ploughshares, "Childless"
Prairie Schooner, "Weights and Measures" and "Vassar's Vincent"
Salamander, "From the Curious Cabinets of Rosamond Purcell,"
Sea Change, "Urban Genesis"
Soujourner: The Women's Forum, "Confessional"
Sou'wester, "Little Murders Everywhere"
The Straddler, "For the Sin of Gossip," "For the Sin of Bossiness," "For the Sin of Passiveness"
West Branch, "At the Other End"

Special thanks to David Barber, Gail Mazur, and John Skoyles, my teachers from Emerson College, where this book began; to Don Bogen and Joanie Mackowski of the University of Cincinnati; and to my first poetry teacher, Max Regan. Also to my especially generous readers, Hadara Bar-Nadav, Andrea Cohen, and Leslie Harrison, and to poets James Lyndon Smith and Adam Day. This book would not have been possible without the support of so many writer friends, including my students and colleagues at Grub Street. Much gratitude also to the New York State Summer Writers Institute, Virginia Center for the Creative Arts, Sewanee Writers' Conference, and The Writers' Room of Boston for their valuable support. And to my family and to Meg Kelley, without whom this book would not have been.

Contents

I

II

III

I

SONG OF THE RATTLING PIPES

Sometimes the house around her sings back,
oil heat clanking against the steel
in low industrial tones—a workers' march,
a miners' rag, muffled mutinies.

She answers, words drumming
their way into the plumbing
of her body, her veins a vessel for song,
blood-coursed vowels, consonance

carrying her up out of her body,
as if she were not pinned
beneath another's weight.
Steam whistles and spouts the melody

of her chorus: *A apocalyptic,*
B bayou, C cerebellum, D detritus—
she falls into the alphabet of possibilities—
F fallacy, G Galapagos, H hovering—

letters an incantation, a portal from her body,
rhythm lifting her up in a circle
of sound: *Z zinnias, A arabesque,*
B braille, until the house falls into silence, the lull
where the sun waits for the sleeping world.

CHILDLESS

Bones like a bird's you quicken
your hands, flit and mock,

take stock of who's watching—
every move a melodrama, a poised

snap, a shot that shapes you
as the lead of a film no one

can stop. Your fingers
play invisible keyboards,

your toes point, turn out
in stance, your dancer's

neck stretches up out of age
and you prattle like a primped-up

little girl. Tip-tapping through
aisles, you smile at the young

man stocking cans, your hands
feeling for the matches you pocketed

at lunch when you took a bite and loudly
sang a hungry cluck:

it's too much, it's too much.
The waiter blushed and

Mother, suddenly I was hungry,
wanted to consume the bread,

the wine, the table, the flowers.
the salt shaker, the chairs.

WEIGHTS AND MEASURES

If the measure of a man is always set
by lengths on another man's body,
how can I be measured
in feet, the long toe of a King's death
shortening me once, history
constantly clipping and stretching me?

What choice do I have
but to fit the bar in Sèvres, marked?
To be held against heights
of the permanent, fixed, hard?
My body metered. Made to matter to the gram.

An ax swings as heavy
as the wood it breaks, and when uprooted
bees swarm, their honey becomes
a cup, a pint, a quart.
But the scale does not discern
between clover and sweetness
for a finer palate.

And yet these are your standards,
official though they may be.
You always take me in your hands
and try to tell me to the ounce.

MIRE

Hail the world of the head:
bucket-heavy,
a hollow swamp.

Thoughts land in bogs
where cattails reign over rocks
left colorless until the rising level
rinses them plum,
bluebell bright.

Light slits the thick air.
Beetles float across the pond,
mirror to the redwing
blackbird singing there.

Pitcher plants
(carnivorous, red)
swallow black flies,
and eyes
of the little brown snake
wait.

Genderless marshlands,
tender minerals:
the earth
recreates inside of us,
multiplying misdemeanors
and falls.

While skin moves around it all
like a worn down puppet,
language tricks
to explain it.

And still, thoughts
(rubber boots) (a boat)
make their moves.

MANUAL ALPHABET

A pair of young lovers sign.
His fingers spell "build" by mounting

skyward like the sparrow's hop up
branches and eaves.

Her hands break
an invisible stick in two.

On a building site in Mexico, a boy's
hands are full, so his lips twitch and point

as an American girl watches – fetch,
nails, there – she reads

his facial patterns, common language
made over hammer and drill.

Each gesture a sign for the differing
labors of want and wonder.

He loves her.
She brings him nails.

FOR THE SIN OF GOSSIP

Nine solemn pigeons take over the bench,
preside over the punishment of those
about whom they've heard the best bits.
The jury disrupts arguments with song—
their cooing drowns the carping claims of long burnt
tail feathers: the fat plaintiff covers his ears.
There is no shortage of evidence.
This is the court of the pigeons who scout
out scandal from the tattlers who
put their beaks to the word on the street,
every billing becoming a buried brief.
Can you hear them calling your name?
What haven't they seen on their flights behind
our bushes or to our windowsills?

FOR THE SIN OF BOSSINESS

Queen of the Bees, your hum builds hives,
bores a buzz in the hearts of drones.
Your stinger stuns your last week's rival
and sends her spiraling to the hay.
All the pretty boys listen from above
the stalls; they hate for you to call their name.
This stable your palace where you command
workers at your feet or out on flowered streets.
Why does it all sound like honey on your tongue?
Your venom entombed in combs, you never leave
but reign over the fields your workers keep
while you complain of them and sleep.
The horses swat their tails, swipe as flies flit by.
They don't even hear your little bee-speak.

DIALECTIC

First Lines from Ricardo Piglia

We yearn for a more primitive
language than our own,

but take in words with metered grace,
swallow the garments they've worn.

Mimic sounds, imagine
we are known, comprehensible.

City, I say, granite
forming in my mouth. *City*,

you agree, glass blooming
blue in iridescent shards.

Mammoth, I explain, woolly
and exact. *Mammoth*, you exclaim,

dreaming places greater than
an unmapped universe.

And so we translate each other's wills
from subjunctives and indicatives.

One wanting the other, the other wanting
what is absent.

Ears pressed to the ink, we pause
and the echo turns the phrase.

REPERTOIRE

Sasha says the most beautiful sound
    in the world is the sound
        of a neuron dying–

a note that strikes her, a scientist
    of some years, with sorrow
        when the ensuing silence hits.

Male birds birth new neurons
    so they can expand
        their song repertoire

to reel in a mate: the female
    mockingbird likes a match
        full of tunes,

so her suitor's brain swells
    with them in October,
        has let them die by June.

We humans try to keep
    our limited stash:
        our breeding is song-free

except for the occasional rockstars
    of youth, the pied pipers
        with their pull

on the young girl's dreams. We
    don't create simply
        to mate.

Sasha penetrates the animal brain,
    studies its reactions
        to sounds electrifying the screen:

but it's not Bach, or pop
      or rock, or hummed hymns
            that make the brain respond.

She listens until the neuron dies,
      then grieves for the answers
            it can no longer give.

What is it like to love
      a neuron,
            to be loved like that?

To skewer one for the love
      of something larger,
            something larger than a you,

a me, a hardwired brain
      that keeps bringing us back
            to the search for the beloved?

CELESTIAL MECHANICS

I have been betrayed by gravity;
it does not connect me to anything.

Sometimes I am floating in a tower, unreachable.
My hands pressed cold against the glass.

I see you floating by: a lost skyscraper, an unwinged vessel,
the moon.

For years, I calculated my orbit by yours.
Or was I fooled by that too?

There are larger pulses at work.
The trains grumbling beneath the surface,

the kicked surge of the power plant as two million
eyes open, two million feet fall.

RAILROAD APARTMENT

Orange light moves across the façade,
reveals record of the dash, the smash
of spectacle lens on glass. Gone
is the slight scheme of waiting:
wrecked wheel on a platform, broken teeth
found behind the old stove, the light
fixtures blinking in the missing hallways.
Now the last car chugs
out, a caboose without remorse.
Feet drumming wooden floors, waxy
smile of open windows, a scream, a falling
screen. As if the clean-swept skull cracks
any unforeseen delays. But here
the end opens back to the entrance.
O circular doors, taking you back
to the moment before.
Leave now the alleyway sings.

HABITAT

Sore and dumb, bumbling
    like a skunk
        wandering among the dogs

in a city neighborhood at dusk
    on the cusp of
        autumn with its tender

turn toward everything you fear:
    a wind that steels you,
        the hard Charles

River glinting, thousands
    of young faces filling
        the streets, alleys, bars.

The couples with their hands on waists
    and shoulders
        or clasped in laughter.

No one sees your weathered
    frame bolstering
        itself in the breeze.

You slip-step caution as you inhale
    habit, history, the city
        that kept your youth.

URBAN GENESIS

Clay makes muddy limbs
    and hollows.
A sheltered stand of sinking

roots, the river's pleasured
    act of vanishing–
this magician's tricks

leave nothing but
    a stick where a willow
or an oak stood, where

the land was once dry
    and even, yielding
grass and fixing rocks

as if they were permanent history.
    Burnt wings
and split bones

aren't the only archaeologies
    that float.
Plastic duck, the flute that's rusted,

keys that can't open
    anything anymore.
In the deep there are houses

where even the drawers
    are filled with mud.
No excavation will release

the inscribed books, histories
  of correspondence,
sheaths of hand-scrawled poems,

loose black and white faces
  still grinning
through the muck and dark.

WHEELS

Go ahead, reinvent the wheel.
Make it vertical, make it a circular train,

an air-born gondola.
Light up the world's fair

with a fifty-cent ride.
Let the bodies fly high.

The body becoming the wheel
is nothing new.

In India, the spokes are ribs
arched upward, opening

like an accordion. You
stand on your palms and soles,

your navel an axle pressed tightly
up above the pump and drum

of blood rush, a rage against
weighted bones and skin.

You become an ancient torturer's
device, the lathe, Fortune's turn,

rolling wheel, rusted wheel, Catherine wheel
sparking into broken spokes.

LOCAL CARNIVAL

A man is pounding nails into his face.
Finding the holes in his skull.

The crowd fills with tattooed ladies
and the bearded babies cry.

He knows where he is missing.
His pregnant belly hangs in leather.

The crowd jeers and someone
throws a penny candy.

He whirls the drill and drives
the bit into his beak.

The crowd yawns,
waits for the next act.

Backstage, he'll pull them out.
Bloodless luck, again.

FOR THE SOLITARY DINER

I love you. I love nobody.
I love the way the storm is coming down,
sky against ground, and my electric driven
bones begin to ache and the harpist
across the hall plays out our melancholy.

I love nobody. I love you. Whoever
you are walking up the stairs past my floor or on the street
down below where umbrellas fill and collapse,
collapse and fill. I love every rickety
framework that fills with wind, that holds for you.

I love nobody. There is nobody
to love and yet I still love you, whoever
you are sitting on the subway beside me,
or setting off the bells that sing to me
from a distance, wherever you are, my fate
my melody, my untapped figure. My nobody, my you.

I love you, I love nobody. I love you every time
I see you leaving the theater alone, or spooning
your soup with solitude in the café. I see you
in every part of the city I trespass through.
How could I not, you, the ones
I could love, you, the yous,
the millions of you, the nobodies.

CITYSCAPE

This is the bruise of the city,
 the mark across our faces
  when we rise from tunnels

gasping in the next opening of doors,
 only to find another sealed gate
  and another and another,

circling around the narrow
 streets that once
  knew ground.

This is the sound the city sings:
 rattle of the metal cage, songs of mice
  scuttling near the third rail,

everything in one white vanish
 whispered by the search
  of crumb to crumb.

These cities are reliefs
 carved in sinking hills
  or built up from landfill.

Bricks of blood now drained
 to dull concrete blocks:
  the civilized world.

II

LITTLE MURDERS EVERYWHERE

As for me, I was merely an accessory:
I raised the ax and chopped the frozen squirrel in thirds.

The red-tailed hawk watched me
marble-eyed,

our fear strung as taut as the line that joined us.
When I offered her the unwanted –

tiny beaks, spindly legs (male chicks from the factory)–
she came to me, swallowed them whole, left

not a trace of yellow in my covered palm.
Our rope never loosening the length between us.

I tried to please her, found corpses everywhere,
scraped them from the pavement, then

transported, froze, and butchered them.
Small birds, two chipmunks,

a pregnant field mouse. A rattlesnake.
Dark-blood bodies, casualties I didn't mourn.

I loved only her, her snapping severed wing,
that vicious grip, her equivalent of a fist.

And what could she think of me?
I was the dark room, the leather glove, the rope.

CONFESSIONAL

I am married to grief,
    to the dull hammer
        pounding my lover's skull.

Premeditated loss drives
    my daily tasks, the juggling
        of pills and forms:

fill out name, fill out
    invasions of the body, slash
        the mark next to single

as if I do not exist on the bed,
    the bathroom tiles, or up
        the slow stairs.

I am the leper: death's stain
    runs everyone off, as if my
        impending loss might mark them.

I am familiar among the aged spouses
    of waiting rooms.
        She hands him his cane,

remembers his coat. And I put my keys in the teacup,
    or pour the water on the plate, already
        practicing the art of forgetting.

AFTERMATH

Fort Sewall, Marblehead Harbor

We are waiting, weary to the sound of relentless bees, worried
by the distant light, the storm's augury.

The disease has yielded an aftermath, another prognosis.
Dilapidated—that is how we would be described today,

moored with the other old boats, while out in the storm
a crew attacks their supper heartily.

Black bees burdened with stolen gold police the lawn
where we wait—our bodies stretched across the grass—

for night, its hosts of fireflies a casing for light
when we most need it.

We are thirsty, surrounded by water heavy with salt.
We are hungry for the chatter of crickets, some anthem of waiting.

The weighted clap of the sky. And then, only darkness.

WATERSHED

Eyes, almond colored, open to the gesture of rain,
close to the crash: smashed drops, freezing northwest rain.

Architecture of bones, roof of skin –
these set no foundations for the chiseling rain.

When lilac crouched at the brick of your newfound home,
rail ties were hard beneath your body, and slick with rain.

A sundial ticks silence in a garden masked as lot;
here we watch new shoots, weighted, wrestle the rain.

No one returns to the streets you call your own,
now washed out, condemned. Gutted by rain.

One by one, crickets join in the chorus,
hail the passing of the dark bearing, possessed rain.

And here you are on the pavement, Morgan, dry,
lamenting even as the petals open in the absence of rain.

AN EVERYDAY DISASTER

The moment I fell through the floor
I wasn't even thinking of you.
The faded brown and yellow linoleum
had always held me before. Hadn't hinted
at the decaying foundation: years of neglect,
shoddy workmanship, carpenter ants.
The floor had never sighed beneath my weight,
shown hesitation, or weakness.
I was caught in an everyday act, a step,
and suddenly my leg gave way,
as if to fall from me—
my body followed in disbelief,
sinking until my head leveled
with the toilet bowl. There was less sound
than I would have imagined, but who
would imagine that? I had never
even liked that cabin, never
realized that I expected anything of it.
You would have said it was just
a simple matter of rotten wood,
but I had to ask why did I ever believe
the floor would hold me?

FOR THE SIN OF TWO-TIMING

You love silken sides of a racehorse in sweat—
a win greeted by cheers, a raucous rise
from the bleachers where even the small child
fingers the change in his pocket, willing
to bet on it all again. Why wouldn't you
put your money on the dark-eyed beauty,
her untamed kick and gait, her red-saddled sheen?
Who wouldn't fall for the muscled glory of her?
In the throes of her gallops you forget
your own pony's ribs rising against the flesh,
those first slow circles around the corral.
You neglect her daily patience, always
waiting for the carrot, your hand, the lead.
The sure-footed love she wants to give you back.

FOR THE SIN OF LYING

She folds orange paper into tiny cranes,
a pair of wings for every lie. One hovers
on the windowsill, trembling in spring wind.
Another on the stove watches flames rise,
ready to wrap around its thin and fragile throat.
The cranes swarm the bed, staining the white like
a field of poppies ready to bloom,
each pod a vessel portending doom.
She has marked them all for her revenge,
dreams nightly of a massacre, of truth.
The want of which now keeps her awake:
she knows no footprints will be left
by the executioner's smooth shoe.
Nameless as he wrings the little folded necks.

FILM REVIEW

Lace-petticoat-layered past stitches up the leg
    of a love worn
lorn, and hands flit over bright-stained terrain,

carefully dyed with barberry, pomegranate,
    walnut, sassafras,
tumeric, onion skin, the thin peelings of a carrot.

An incongruous stew or the stain for a cloth
    shoe set to step
into a ticketed-out waltz, a wind-down duet.

Pairs skittle and scuttle into hallways and verandas,
    disappear beyond trees
sinking some grass stains into the knock-kneed kisses.

Bliss of a ball, tall clock strike, the socks sink
    down to the ankles
and the next day dims the world with no horizon.

Some sort of lickety-split love, a pigeon morphed
    from mourning dove—
carriers of inky words, the line earnestly observed.

Bit lip and bawled, the scrawled apology etches in
    ruin, torrent, wind
and moors: still begging *dance, dip, adore.*

EROS IS HEADED TOWARDS US

Golden or lead. Love or indifference.
Although Eros has been close, it's no threat
to hit us. Landing on Eros is no cakewalk.
Scientists are delighted by Eros.
Sappho says he's sweetbitter.
Eros is solid and primitive, far
from being smooth. Dominated by dust–
covered impact craters, scattered rocks.
The chapters of Eros are short.
Eros seizes and shakes from execution
of a controlled descent to its surface.
If you stood on Eros, you'd make a nice footprint.
If love should love, love would be an asteroid.
Asteroids are more subtle than we imagined.

EVEN THE GALAXIES

The world is in love without me.
I'm not sure how I missed it,

the day when the daffodils swooned
over the recycling bin

and the dump truck married
the smallest house on our block.

I must have walked by
three fire hydrants arm-in-arm

with a mail carrier, a Great Dane
and a tomato plant, respectively.

When the office windows worshiped
the traffic light at 5th and Pearl, and the parkway

danced off with its fiancée, the candy
factory, I was blind. No, I didn't notice

when two neighboring states eloped,
or the Indian Ocean had an affair

with the Atlantic
and with the Baltic Sea.

Even a few galaxies coupled up
during the early days of August.

And now, here I am, watching.
What do I know?

The way the sea should have loved me,
but didn't? The way this small bee

circles me, darts off, stings the stray cat's nose
and dies in bacchanalian ecstasy?

HUSBANDRY

We were driving by the Heavy Equipment Operation
Vocational Education site—an overgrown field, fallow
and waiting to be driven down in futile circles by fits
and starts of a stalled engine. Across the street, the Institute
for Animal Husbandry's parking lot was empty, save
for a compact car topped with a right-side-up canoe,
which we agreed was upside down. I was staring out windows,
cataloguing you as another failure in a long line:
the park ranger who knew every mushroom in the forest,
the poet, the painter, the sailor, the Peace Corps volunteer,
the failed Olympic cyclist, the drummer who left a band
before it became big: all the wrong vocations. The engineer
had been no better. Nor the actor turned theater historian,
and I started to wonder if a little heavy machinery
needed to be thrown into the mix. I asked you to turn around
and pull into the lot, where I crawled up over the hood
of the car and began to bail the boat out with my hands.
Hours passed. You watched me from your sedan
while I scooped out the last inches, picked up the oars and began
to row away, paddling through air toward open field,
where I trailed a choppy backhoe making figure eights, and then
dipped up and down in the shadow of a standstill crane.
I didn't look back to see if you were still there. I imagined
rowing back to the Institute, where I'd meet a horse whisperer
and a large-animal vet with a chimp's heart, and I'd watch
while they mated two animals with the same vocation: no
competition, just paid-for farm sex. Getting the job done.

FOR THE SIN OF FOOLISHNESS

Love is a false god, a masked fraud
that even the atheist courts with belief.
A magician favored for his sleight of hand.
We love to be fooled. We follow
a trail of circumstantial evidence
built by other blind believers. Why doubt
what even the godless hold pure? Each moment
in love's grasp takes us further from reason.
And when it's proven absent, not even leaving ash?
We perform our ablutions, place pennies and lockets
on its altar, search the faces of people on the train.
Oh Love, we whisper from the streets—
make me a follower, make me care for no other
but you: the enemy, the savior, the absent
plea, the adored and ageless fallacy.

III

FROM THE CURIOUS CABINETS OF ROSAMOND PURCELL

Wing in one, tongues in two and three.
Dressed fleas. The riddled trio
of animal, vegetable, mineral—

(a calcified nesting egg.)
And the forged specimens,
like the striped egg nature abhors,

but which lies in the dusty glass light
as the lucky lens opens.
Scientists' kingdoms materialize

in remnants of the human hand
closed in covers of human skin.
Captured curiosities, like the buttons

engraved with slaves' names.
Buttons someone kept making,
someone kept shining, year after year.

INFESTATION

Ghostlike, they came to me
through open windows, cracked doors.

Shed their husks, left them hollow
and opalescent on the sill, left

a buzzing breath, their small bodies
remembered on my skin.

Strange, their lack of warmth,
despite their blood,

and the ease with which a life
is cut in flight.

Yes, I took lives every day in desperation—
a wild germ of hatred, not solely fear.

I too had a murderous side,
some poisonous self seeping

into me, slowly building.
But they were stealth in their approach—

letting me think I controlled
them from my little dark doorway.

When it was they who flooded my room
and wakened me from my life.

THE POLITICIAN'S WIFE

You inhabit my throat,
    play me like a flute, fingering
        my chest with sounds

so jasmine sweet
    I choke and want
        to dissect them, to knife

the untruths I parrot to the world,
    mouthing the same refrains
        you've taught me.

My aria gasps
    only from your bellows,
        your lips still as bone.

Someday I will lift my tongue,
    press it against
        your durable words,

and spit the syllables back
    until sounds vibrate
        my own stalled motor.

A slow hum rumbling
    ricocheting
        against you, my love.

AT THE OTHER END

It's the old form of telephone crying like a bell,
no one at the other end. The messages delayed
by thirty years. I'm tired of you, America. America,
where are you? I can finally hear you.
My steps on you like a metronome.
Everything I hear is amplified. Records
and eight tracks, a cassette playing your name,
some lost song, the words I can't make out.
Minutes snapped over the wrist. My mind's
a museum of what I've heard: radio static,
vacuums, hairdryers, the man pursing his lips
at the gym. It all makes me cringe.
When they put these in my ears, the technician
turned the dials and I cowered
at the sounds of the city. I'd kept the world
at bay for decades, and now it screeched at my feet
with its hums and rings and whistles and shrieks.
Where was I to look? I'd read faces for years.
Trying to hear your eyes, your mouth's crease.
I can read a body like a book.
My long pauses, the lack of a smile: me, listening
with my face. It exhausts me, trying to hear
the world breathe and speak. Missing, always,
what whispers: sweet nothings, sly comments. Dull, slow,
the way your words slug their way to my brain.
Or rather the guesses I make to replace what wanders off.
This is what the crowd does to me. This is what I miss
in every whisper. My body is the old telephone, the old
bell ringing at me— me, far away, at the other end.

FOR THE SIN OF FORGETTING

You're keeper of this ill-fated miser
with his top hat and cane dance.
You watch your old man's last tricks, his
dementia performed. You cannot forget
the leather strap, his bow ties, his golfing cap.
Do you mock his senility, dress it in the joke
of a family cabaret? Or do you envy him
in the checkout line, his feet tapping?
You hate his moth-eaten vestiges of play,
fight back at his antiquated order, do nothing
to keep the wooden wheel from spinning right
into flames on the electric track. You envy
his childhood staged before you. You want
to do it all again, want to see the world made new.

FOR THE SIN OF PASSIVENESS

Oh little whippet, oh little whine
and curse, my shadow self.
You want to turn pedestrians on their heels
and startle souls out of everyone
you snap at, to howl like a siren
unresisted, to create more than mistake.
You long for a life better than a litter,
a soft paw. You'd like to awe and allure—
to transform into the beast that frightens you
more: it's the coyote, the lion, the bear,
you adore. No one can destroy
what locks up fear inside you.
You think you're in a steel box waiting
for a passerby to set you free.

VASSAR'S VINCENT

*I hate this pink-and-gray college. If there had been a college
in Alice in Wonderland it would be this college.*

Edna St. Vincent Millay, 1914

Rumor has it she jumped
        from the high windows of Jewett Hall,
                but I've not seen her there

silhouetting the hard quad,
        haunting my daily path. Instead,
                I find her laughing:

she hides behind trees that oversee
        Vassar Pond, dodges mellifluous pleas,
                whisperings of her name,

Vincent! Vincent! Where are you? Yes,
        I hear her lovers' calls, silvered songs
                of young girls, hands clasped,

devotions on slips slid beneath doors
        and into weighty volumes of Latin
                and Greek. I hear her sly

denouncements muffled in frail teacups
        and other vessels she spills over. Too
                large for these ivy-covered walls,

the library built for Gods and Kings, turrets
        curved around modest skirts
                and crossed ankles.

A factory for wives? A parenthetical
        brilliance for the female mind before
                tuck and pleat and bottles of defeat?

She tosses her head, her luminous, ghostly head,
        and whispers in young girls' ears, tapping us
                towards the stacks, to the tomes
                where she never sleeps.

RESIDENTIAL

Even the mansion gets lonely in the expansive yard,
wants to fill its own rooms with tsotchkes and burdens.

Looks out every window, breathes in, breathes out.
Waits for the knock on the door.

Forgets the series of pipes that connect it, the wires
little pulses like veins

to neighboring houses, fenced looming plants, the stewing
sewage pools, the high wire act of poles and lines.

It's the garage that's powerless, free-standing,
clutching old junk like a sentimental ex-lover.

Waiting for someone to drive in, park.
Waiting to breathe in the leftover fumes.

GEMINI

They were held under water for three days, breathless
beneath the current, and when they rose, skin white, petal-bare,

there was a haunting on the shore, a whisper
falling from the branches.

They were trapped under water for three nights,
those waiting gasps, and when they'd risen,

no one was listening for angels, for ghosts
of children who'd been knotted to the underground

roots until the late summer floods
birthed them back up to sky.

Their bodies were found, but they lingered
on the shore, crept into the bordering woods, shadowed

by the rumor that they had been twins, joined in those last moments,
reincarnated now into the myths of the cypress, the swamp's

low waters thick with weeds, that cold and thrilling
chill that lures children back into the deep.

AFTER VIETNAM

Didn't you lose your boyhood here
along the ditch, once,
where monkey flowers gild the roadside?
Didn't it spill into the fields and bloom?
The river moved towards your footsteps.
This was not like catfish eyes
staring back at you in solitude, the trophy
of a long day's catch. These were green frogs
as small as your thumbnail.
There was nowhere else to walk
but on thousands of heartbeats.

NOTES TO THE SCIENTIST

Powdered sugar snows
over the world
of a thousand white husk flies.

You watch them die,
marking the natural body count.
Death by sweet beauty.

Then you brew a poisonous
storm, a chemical flurry,
and drop it on a thousand more.

Delicate flakes flutter,
weight on wings
spinning through the air.

You ask, how much can we take?
We, with our bodies
not so unlike the fly.

There is no hospice,
no priest, no mourning.
Your formulas and graphs

their only record
as the storm draws closer
to our own dense and questioning bodies.

I ask, was the poison just as beautiful,
those delicate flakes alighting on wings,
spinning through the air?

PAST DUE

The tarred bird binds the chokecherry to the stem,
gold and silver fish swim through cascades and cuts
of rock which stop the flow and leave them belly-up–

this luck of a pass has passed: the fast-down trees
brown in disease, the rot stench begins its seasonal
pinch, and the whole valley sighs. It's been forty years

since the trucks first came, eighty since the train, and
here again, the headstones gather slime and guts,
each past sinking until they move the whole gang

over to a smaller city's lot, and mother of mothers,
mother's brother, the other side of the family tree,
each of them will have to be removed. Here's how we pay

up front, as well as past due. Everyone else's lives
a cost to this one time round. They left a sticker
on the house, the car, the gravestone: your life

has been recalled and the dead must be renewed.
It's no wonder the mold is turning blue, the sky
orange. It's the dead, churning, nowhere else to go.

HOW TO SKIN A SWAN

First, defeather, one by one, removing
flight. Deconstruct the illusion of white,
note the muddied feathers, the mites.
The buried ebony quills plucked from
the pink and bubbled skin. Then, drain
slowly from the heart. There mustn't be
a drop left to stain or moisten. Slice
carefully down the center; split clean
the floating body. The throat will be
difficult—the ghostlike trumpeting
echo means the skin may be tougher
than its delicacy implies. Dye it dark,
tailor it well. When you see beauty,
you must want to remove it.

RESCUER

We rely on the bridge to hold us up –
stalwart steel beams bolster us
as our faith glides over a glaze

of asphalt, unbreakable.
As if on prairie, hard dirt,
an endless earth to cradle us.

Who expects collapse, or
the disaster of a silhouette
swinging into the air off the edge?

Or this– a man has tossed his children
in: they fall like rocks, one, two, three,
four lives into the bitter deep.

Now the divers forage for remains,
for bodies to bury in drier lands.
And still, there is a mother,

and still, the bridge moves under
the rumble of trucks and cars
loaded with boats and bikes,

and still the hand reaches under
the dark murk you gazed in once,
imagining your own life breaking

through the surface of ice,
imagining a parallel life
below, where silence stills

itself and mutes the traffic
above. Still, the hand reaches down
as if to find, up as if to be saved.

CITY MORNING

The monkey house wakes up
the neighborhood with a call and response

not unlike the whoops of homecoming night:
hollow, incessant, hard to decipher the edge

between joy and lament. The other team has scored
a point. The zookeeper is out of bananas.

They have no species in the early morning hours
from blocks away. How could I have confused

an orangutan and a lemur? A gorilla and a macaque?
We walk closer and they have names

their parents never chose. Their extended
families have fallen out of touch.

The children are placing their hands on the glass.
The monkey's breath fogs it up in return.

They're silent when we circle them.
They chew and stare.

Later, they too will hear the neighborhood –
dusk's calls for children, nightfall's moans and fights.

We're each other's misplaced habitats.
Calling out into the city's rising and falling light,

hoping someone will hear. Each thinking
we've made them just like us.

THE BLESSING OF THE ANIMALS

The first came to me like a chalk dog
on the sidewalk, barked back
at my hand that tried to sketch in
the missing parts.

The second licked my wrist,
slid in retreat to his shell.
His back bore the dry wound
of an inkless tattoo.

The third was a vapor
admitted through the chapel's cracks.
He passed through our lungs, dissipated
beneath my attempts to anoint him.

The fourth was a tornado—
pummeled the pews, slammed
Mary from her niche-nicked saints
scuttling in to heal the shards.

This was not all. There were flocks,
schools, herds, charms,
rhumbas, and swarms.
The sanctuary fluttered and breathed.

I was no exception.
I knelt before myself and wept.

Photo: Mara Brod

REBECCA MORGAN FRANK's poems have appeared in *Blackbird, The Georgia Review, Guernica, Ploughshares, Prairie Schooner, Best New Poets 2008,* and elsewhere, and she was awarded the Poetry Society of America's 2010 Alice Fay di Castagnola Award. She is co-founder and editor of the online magazine *Memorious.*